Good-bye Working Mom Syndrome
From One Working Mom to Another.

By Leigh Martin

21 ways to help minimize the guilt and help you appreciate the fact that millions of other women feel the same way.

Strategic Book Group
Durham, Connecticut

Strategic Book Group
P.O. Box 333
Durham CT 06422
www.StrategicBookClub.com

ISBN 978-1-60976-668-9

Printed in the United States of America

This book is dedicated to all the working moms
trying to keep everyone happy.

Hello working mom,

We all know that being a mom is a full-time job. Being a working mom is like juggling two full-time jobs on a limited schedule while trying to keep your sanity. Why is there only twenty-four hours in a day? It's also one of the greatest tests of patience as you continually attempt to try and keep everyone around you happy (maybe even yourself, if you're lucky). Notice that I didn't mention anything yet about the guilt we all feel trying to make it all work.

Women before us fought for equal rights. We wanted to be able to stand up for ourselves and voice our opinions. Now, we are able to vote. We wanted to be able to prove that women can do a job just as well as a man can or even better. Now, we are able to compete with them at almost every job opportunity. We wanted to be able prove to the world that women can handle working out of the home while raising a family. Now, millions of women prove this around the world on a daily basis.

Of course, all of these successes also have come with a lot of pressure, a lot of stress, and some failures. So, who do we complain about this to? No one. There's no way we want people to know that we're struggling trying to juggle our work and home life.

There is hope, working mom. There are millions of women out there in your situation. Okay, maybe not in your exact situation, but other women who can relate with what you're going through. And sometimes, that's all you need to hear ... that you're not the only one trying to make it work.

Who better to offer you suggestions on how to help improve your juggling act then a working mom herself? These suggestions, along with personal stories as well as those shared by other working moms, may actually make you feel a little better about yourself and give you a fresh perspective on a working mom's life.

Enjoy and don't be afraid to pass this book along to other working moms out there who may feel overworked, underappreciated, and a little stressed out.

Remember . . . it could always be worse!

Cheers,

Leigh

TABLE OF CONTENTS

INTRODUCTION

Life Happens.

"Hurry up! Let's go; we're going to be late. No, don't do that. Get your coat on. What do you mean you have to poop? Now? Can't it wait?"

Once the kids are ready finally to get going out the door, you quickly do a snot check on each shoulder. No snot; it's a good morning.

You load the kids up; check to make sure the house door is locked and that you remembered your cell phone, purse, and daily "To Do" list. Check, check, check! You take one deep breath before backing out of the driveway. It's looking like a great morning.

You rush to the sitter's, run your kids into the house, and quickly undress them. You update her on medications, rashes, and nap times. You forget once again to bring her more diapers. You promise her that you'll bring them tomorrow and make a mental note to add them to your list. (You appreciate that at least the sitter is kind enough not to roll her eyes until you leave the house). You're out the door in 7.5 minutes. There's no screaming or crying as you leave. What a super morning.

As you're driving to work, you glance down at your "To Do" list flapping on the front dashboard by the radio. Okay, pick the kids up right after work and then rush like hell for the baby's needles. That should take about an hour. That's just enough time to get home, make something for supper, and then hurry over to the soccer field for your four-year-old son's first practice of the season!

Now, what is on the menu for supper tonight . . . chicken? Nah, takes too long. Roast beef? Oh, that would've been good if only you had thought of throwing it in the crock pot this morning. Curse that snooze button you hit too many times this morning. You blame the fact that the baby was up way more than usual last night. (It's as if he knew he was getting those blasted needles today.) Realistically, that snooze button would've probably been pushed the same number of times anyway. Regardless, spaghetti it is! It's quick and you know everybody will eat it without complaining. As a bonus, it's also easy enough to clean up before soccer!

Oh, crap! You just remembered that there's also a Parent Council Meeting tonight at 7:30 at your son's school. You guess you could probably skip it, but being the vice president, you want to stay updated on what's going on. Okay, time to add to your game plan. Your husband should be home from work by the time you all get home from soccer tonight, so he should be able to watch the kids and put them to bed. Now, you'd better make sure they have their baths before you leave the house; otherwise, Dad will just put them to bed in whatever they're wearing, spaghetti sauce and all. And that stuff is not fun to wash off the next morning. Oh, and you might as well give the kids' their medication before leaving. They've been trying to fight off their ear infections for a week now. And you know that if you don't do it, Dad will somehow manage to *forget* to do it. Then, you'll be stuck trying to get them to take it while they're half asleep when you get home.

You also notice that there's some kind of work-related scribble on your list. Darn, you know there's that project that has to get done by next week. When will you have time to work on it at home? Tonight is not a good night, and tomorrow doesn't look good either. You're definitely going to have to scratch that off your list (for today anyway).

Maybe working through your lunch hour tomorrow will help you get caught up. It's not like you actually want to use your lunch hour to eat (note the sarcasm).

You decide to stop thinking about your "To Do" list and crank up the radio. Maybe that'll help drown out the little voice inside you that doesn't seem to shut up. You also try singing and bobbing along to the music for good measure, which feels great, but it also makes the couple parked alongside you look twice while waiting for the red light to change.

Okay, working mom, take a breather! Who hasn't had these thoughts before? With not enough time on your hands and too many things on your plate, sometimes your workdays feel a little overwhelming no matter how organized and prepared you are.

You work and you're expected to maintain a happy household at home every day. You know you love your husband, you know you love your kids, and you know you love your job (well maybe *love* is a strong word), but sometimes all you want to do is scream and vent to somebody about your troubles. You must learn to appreciate the fact that other women are going through these same daily struggles.

Good-bye Working Mom Syndrome offers situations you can relate to as well as suggestions that will help make your life more manageable. There's always something you can learn or change to help you cope. Most importantly, you can't take things so seriously; life is too short!

From one working mom to another; relax, enjoy, and laugh. If you can't relate to the material in this book (even just a little), then obviously you're not a working mom.

Making Life Easier
Tip #1–It's Okay to Cry.
First Day Back

"I can do it. I can do it. I can do it," you mumble to yourself softly under your breath as you wake up extra early from an uneasy night of sleep. It's your first day back at work and your son's first day at day care. After spending the whole night tossing and turning, your attempt at a good night's rest results in dark circles under your eyes and a pounding headache. You look in the mirror. Great! What the hell were you thinking? You can't do this. You can't go back to work and leave your son with strangers. What if it's not too late? You can still change your mind, right? You can still decide to stay home with him. After a few seconds, you give your head a much-needed reality shake (which really doesn't help your headache), and you start your morning with a cup of hot coffee.

As you sit down to enjoy your morning java, you tell yourself to get a grip. You checked out the day care yourself two weeks ago. You did think that the fees were a little steep, but understandably, that's the "going" rate these days. And you know your son had a good time when you were there because he didn't want to leave when it was time. That's always a good sign; besides, you had a great first impression of the two ladies who will be looking after him. That's the problem: they'll be looking after him and not you! For most of his awake hours in the day, somebody else will be looking after him. They will be looking after him when he takes his first step. They will be looking after him when he says his first words. They will be looking after him when . . . stop it! Stop it! You know you have to stop making yourself sick! You quickly get up from the kitchen table as you finish your coffee and get yourself ready before your son wakes up.

After loading your son's diapers, wipes, bottles, extra clothes, snacks, and everything else on the list you received from the day care they said you needed to bring, you head out the door for your first morning as a working mom. You appreciate how gloomy the sky is as it seems to match your mood as you make your way through morning traffic on your way to day care. Darn, you're thinking you should've left ten minutes sooner. You forgot how hectic rush-hour traffic can be. You make a mental note to leave earlier tomorrow.

You quickly glance at your son in the back seat. He seems oblivious to the fact that he'll be spending most of his day away from you. His constant babbling soothes you a little, and when he gives you that crooked half-smile as you make eye contact in the rear-view mirror, your heart melts. He'll still love you after today; well, you hope so anyway!

After you quickly update the day-care staff of your son's daily routine and eating habits, you decide to give him a quick hug before heading out. Big mistake! You're sure his wailing can be heard from down the street! Darn, why didn't you just stick to your first instinct and sneak out the door. You're sure he sensed that you were leaving him, or maybe it was the look on your face that gave it away. Nevertheless, it takes you a couple of minutes of you crying in your vehicle before getting it together enough to drive out of the day-care parking lot to work.

As you pull into the same staff parking lot you haven't seen in quite a few months, you decide to check yourself out in the rear-view mirror before getting out of the car. Good grief! Your mascara is running, your face is blotchy from crying, and as you look down at the front of your new skirt, you notice snot marks. Oh dear, there's also a snag mark down the back of your nylons from hooking it on the door while rushing out of day care. There's no way nail polish is going to fix this. Good thing you have another pair in your purse. Hey, what don't you have in your purse these days? You'll have to change in the bathroom before work.

After cleaning yourself up a little, you feel a bit better and attempt to walk to your desk without crying. You get mad at yourself and think, *Get it together, it's not the end of the world*! So you start work today. Suck it up, princess! You knew this day would come.

You manage to sneak to your office before anyone sees you, and you have one last meltdown before the workday officially begins. Fortunately, you have to admit that the rest of your day passes fairly quickly and is quite productive.

When 4:30 p.m. rolls around, you're not only the first one out the door; you're also the first one out of the parking lot. Look out, Mario Andretti! You miss your son like crazy and you can't wait to see him. As you whip into the day-care parking, you're unsure as to what kind of greeting you're going to get. You hope he overdoes it with the kisses and hugs. You really do love it when he holds onto your neck like you're his favourite person in the whole world.

You walk in the door and look for him. You see him playing in the corner with his blocks totally focused on trying to pile one on top of the other. He looks over and sees you. He gives you a smile and then continues to play by himself. What the hell? That's not the kind of response you wanted or needed. He's supposed to be ecstatic to see you. He's not supposed to ignore you. You feel the tears well-up in your eyes as you start feeling sorry for yourself. Just as you're about to give up on the grand welcoming, he throws his blocks down and runs over to give you a big hug. Now, that's what you're talking about!

After finding out he had a great day at day care–he ate, he napped, he pooped, he played–you both walk out the door and head for home.

By seven o'clock that evening, you're both thoroughly exhausted. After you manage to pick up the supper dishes, give him a bath, take a bath yourself, and make a little conversation with your husband on how your work day went, you decide to "hit the hay" early. You don't even try to explain to your husband how you were feeling today because there's no way he could understand. You know he can't feel that same guilt when he leaves for work every morning. Or at least, you don't think he does.

You go to sleep with a heavy heart knowing you have to do the same thing tomorrow. You're just hoping it gets easier!

❖

Tip #1–It's Okay to Cry.

Of course it's okay to cry! If someone tries to tell you otherwise, they're either male of have never been in the same situation as you.

There will always be that daily pang of guilt, but the key is not to let it get you down. There are many things you can do to help you cope (which you will learn as you continue to read this book). The first is knowing it's all right to let yourself go ever once in a while. Although, it is probably a good idea to wait until you're by yourself (like in the bathtub) or you may have people, including your husband, thinking you're a depressed, moody woman with PMS. Well, maybe that's not so bad, especially if you want more time to yourself.

Tip #2–Patience, One of the Most Trying Virtues.
The Wrong Pair of Pants

Trying to negotiate with a three year old can be trying. Trying to negotiate with a three year old on a tight schedule is next to impossible, which is exactly the situation you're in this morning. You can't believe it, but you're actually having a face-off with your three year old and you can safely say you're losing the battle.

"I don't wanna wear these pants; I wanna wear the other ones." He stomps his foot on the carpet to prove he's not backing down (you know your husband would say he gets that from you).

"No, you can wear the ones you already have on." You try the firm approach.

"No, I won't. I wanna wear the other ones."

"Look, son. We don't have time this morning. And these pants fit you just right. They used to be your brother's and he wore them all the time." No matter what you say, he knows he's getting to you and you know he's getting to you.

"But Mom, puhleassse! I like the other ones." Okay, time to give in a little if you're planning on getting out the door on time. You've already wasted ten precious minutes on this matter.

"Okay, which other ones do you want to wear?"

"You know, the other pair; the ones I like?" Questioning a three year old can be stressful. You can feel your blood pressure rising a little.

"No, I don't know. Show me." Yeah, like it's going to help having a three year look around. You're starting to get desperate and your patience is wearing thin.

He whines, "Where are they? You know, the ones I like." Oh, boy!

Like you're supposed to know. The ones he liked last week are different than the ones he liked the week before. Lord only knows which pair he's talking about today?

"What colour are they?" You try a different strategy.

"The grey ones. The same as yesterday." Oh, why didn't he say the ones from yesterday? Mind you, it's really your fault since you didn't ask him that specific question. How does that saying go; "Ask and ye shall receive"? You're thinking it should actually say "Ask a three year old the right, specific question and ye shall receive the answer you've been trying to guess for the last twenty minutes!"

"The ones from yesterday are dirty. Mom didn't have a chance to wash them yet."

"But I wanna wear those. You know, the grey ones?"

Okay, if you want to get out the door on time, it's time to do what it takes to get the job done. You pull out his grey sweats from the laundry basket and examine them. Nope, no stains. You hold them up to your nose; they don't smell too bad. You promise you'll give in just this once; otherwise, you'll never get to work on time. After thinking about it, you said the same exact thing last week.

"Okay, you can wear the grey ones." Score one for the three year old.

"Thanks, Mom. I love you." He always seems to know the right time to pull out that phrase.

"I love you, too." You may not love the way he smells in his dirty pants, but you love how his chubby little hands feel around your neck. Then, you look at his chubby little hands. Darn, you're guessing that peanut butter also ended up on the back of your shirt.

As you quickly run out the door five minutes later than usual and after you've changed to peanut butter-free attire, you make a mental note to wash his grey pants tonight. You figure it could prevent another battle tomorrow morning–at least until he opts for a different pair of favourite pants next week.

Tip #2–Patience, One of the Most Trying Virtues.

So what if your son's socks don't match and his shirt is inside out? At least he dressed himself. (Besides, you can always tell people his dad dressed him.)

So what if your husband didn't put the dishes away exactly where they are supposed to go; at least he tried. (Maybe he did it on purpose so you don't ask him again?)

So what if your office at work is not cleaned to your standards even after complaining about it to your boss several times over the past few weeks; at least you're working. (You should have bigger issues to worry about; otherwise, you're obviously not that busy?)

Working mom, you have to learn not sweat the small stuff. Sure, things are not always going to get done the way you like, but your way is not the only way, believe it or not?

Being a working mom is hard enough to manage most days. However, being a constant nagging, working mom could turn you into a bitter, miserable bitch. Who really needs that brought up during the eulogy at her funeral?

"We will always remember Mom as a very hard working, clean, perfectionist. She always liked things done a certain way; her way. We used to joke about her nagging us from the grave. Can you hear her now?"

Just remember that your son would rather hear that he did a good job getting dressed in the morning than to hear you yell at him that he didn't do it right. It will encourage him to keep trying, and that will definitely save you a lot of time in the long run.

Tip #3-Don't Assume.
The Wrong Wedding

Oh boy! How are you ever going to live this down? As you lay in bed recalling the events of the day, you can't help but wonder if this could possibly be the most embarrassing day of your life. Yep, this may actually be talked about for years; no, make that decades to come.

It all started with a little too much on your plate. First, you couldn't say no to your brother-in-law when he asked you to sing at his wedding. You knew it would be a lot of work, but also a lot of fun-especially for a "singing-in-the-shower" type of girl. Of course, it might've helped if you and the other singers had gotten together a lot sooner to practice. Only practising that last week and a half before the wedding really stressed you out.

Secondly, it also would've helped if it wasn't such a busy time at work. The start of a new project always puts you on edge with all the things that have to get done. And your last-minute medical concerns before the wedding were just enough to put you over the limit . . . on top of juggling your two kids at home.

You still don't know how you're going to retell the story to your children and grandchildren of what you did? Well, you'll just start from the beginning.

It's a gorgeous Saturday afternoon as people file out of the church. The wedding ceremony had gone off without a hitch, and everyone was making small talk outside before heading over to the hall where the reception was being held.

Because your youngest son was in the wedding party, along with his dad, you didn't have to worry about them (they were preoccupied taking pictures), and your older son had managed to convince you earlier to let him ride with his cousins to the reception hall. So it was only you–you by yourself. You without anybody else. You alone. It's just so rare to have a little quiet time that you really took the time to enjoy the peaceful ride to the hall feeling relaxed and relieved that the ceremony was over.

Pulling up to the hall, you're happy to find such a great parking stall; only three cars down from what appeared to be the bride and groom's vehicle–a blue SUV. (Hey, you're a woman; it's not your thing to remember the make or model.) And so you were saying, you parked only three cars down from the blue SUV that was parked in front of the hall doors.

After straightening your blouse and skirt, you make your way in and see some familiar faces. You start chatting with them as you line-up at the back of the very long guest-signing line (you know, the one that leads to the gift table and wishing-well cards). As you're standing in line, you're actually kind of surprised by some of the people who are invited to the wedding. You just didn't realize how close some of these people must be to the groom. Or perhaps they were invited from the bride's side. Oh well, that's not your problem. Anything's possible in a small town.

Tired of waiting in line and figuring you have a little pull being the groom's sister-in-law, you excuse yourself and make your way to the gift table. You toss your card in the wishing well and figure you'll sign the guest book later.

As you make your way into the actual seating area, someone gives you a funny look and casually asks you, "Hey, are you at the right wedding? I think your family is at the other hall across town!"

You suddenly stop, turn red while thinking about it, and mutter, "Oh, #@!%, you're right! I *am* at the wrong hall!" You think about slipping out quietly, but not before realizing that you already threw your card in the wishing well. So you graciously excuse yourself once again and make your way to the front of the line. People are really starting to get annoyed with you. Then, you dig through, what seems like the hundreds of cards there, to find yours (okay, maybe there were only dozens). After finding it, you quietly explain that you're at the wrong wedding and get your ass out of there.

You're shaking as you get to your vehicle. You start thinking that you never really looked at the wedding invitation. You never even questioned your husband as to which hall he was going to when he said he was going to help decorate yesterday. You never even thought to ask which hall they had rented. You just assumed that it was the same one most people rented for weddings. Well, that's obvious since you actually knew some people there. So you quickly get the hell out of there and make your way to the other hall across town.

You're still shaking as you enter the right hall. Now, you know you're at the right place since you see your son helping "man" the guest-signing table. Phew! People start asking where you were since you obviously took so long to get there. (*Obviously* must be your favourite word in this story since you obviously ignored the signs that could've prevented you from making this embarrassing mistake.)

You casually make the mistake of mentioning to one guest the reason why you took so long. That is probably the worst thing you could've done. You would've been better off telling them you had diarrhoea and you had to stop a few times along the way there. At least, maybe then, you wouldn't have been the butt of all the jokes throughout the speeches (pun intended). And you couldn't even defend yourself since you didn't have the microphone.

Now who has actually done that? Who has ever shown up to the wrong hall to her own brother-in-law's wedding? It's not even like it was a friend's wedding, which would've been a little more understandable. Really, your own family's wedding?

And what takes the "cake" is that you weren't only the butt of all the jokes at your brother-in-law's wedding, you find out later that they were also talking about you at the other wedding across town. And across town, when it's a small town, is not far enough . . .

Tip #3–Don't Assume.

Of course, the old saying goes: assuming makes an "ass" out of "u" and "me." Now, isn't that the truth? As a working mom, assuming does more harm than good.

You should never assume traffic will be light that morning; leave ten minutes earlier. Also, you should never assume that your boss will understand why you're late one morning while making arrangements for your sick kids; give him a call. You should never assume your husband will understand why you're so tired at night after running around like a mad woman all day; explain some of the things that happened. He may even have some suggestions.

Instead of assuming, be a little more proactive and take that extra step if you need to. Try getting to work ten minutes earlier instead of banking on traffic to go smoothly. Call the office every time you're going to be late and update your husband regularly on what's going on in your life. Sometimes what seems like a little more work will actually lighten your stress load in the long run.

Tip #4–Make a Little "We" Time.
Date Night

You and your husband haven't been out in a while, and you finally have a chance to be alone. As you're driving to a local dine and dance for a worthwhile fundraiser, that little voice in your head starts nattering away. Doesn't it ever shut up?

Did I leave the list of the phone numbers near the phone or by the front door for the babysitter? I told her by the phone, so if I left them at the front door, I'll have to call her and let her know. Let me think. No, I left them for sure by the phone. Phew! That's one less thing to worry about. And did I tell her the snacks were on the cupboard and that the kids shouldn't have water after eight? Crap! Oh well, I'm sure she'll figure out where the snacks are; they are her favourite. And she should remember the "water thing" from last time. And if I have to clean bed sheets tomorrow, so be it. They could use a freshening up anyway! Speaking of freshening up, did I even look in the mirror before leaving tonight? Oh my God, I'd better check my make-up.

As you fiddle through your purse, your husband tries to make adult conversation with you on the way to the party. You have to give him credit for trying.

"I heard they brought in some great door prizes for tonight. That'll really help raise some money. And if the food is good, I'm sure people will be telling their friends to come next year. Hey, are you listening to me?"

Shoot! What did he say? You were too busy searching for the dance tickets in your wallet. So you think maybe you'll try to fake like you were listening. That's nothing he hasn't tried–that's for sure.

"Oh, yeah! Great." You look over at him to try and convince him you know what he said.

Don't forget that after ten years, he knows you well and you can't sell him that vacant look. He plays along.

"Really, you're looking forward to the strippers tonight? I think they expect tips?"

What the hell is he talking about? He starts laughing at your pitiful, disgusted reaction. He got you and you know it. Time to fess up.

"What are you talking about? Strippers? I thought this was a fundraiser. Oh, you . . . Ha! Ha! You got me! I was thinking about where I put the tickets? And I hope everything goes fine at home, I mean. You know the kids are just getting over their colds. You could tell they wanted me at home tonight. Maybe we should just forget this whole thing."

Good thing he won't let you off the hook or let you make all of the decisions; otherwise, you wouldn't go anywhere. He tries once again to convince you that you deserve a break too. He goes through the same spiel almost every time you go out.

"Look, I know you've had a rough week, but you need to get out of the house. The kids will be fine. You'll have fun; you'll see. We haven't seen our friends in so long. You can do a lot of catching up. And I know you like to dance, so maybe we do a little of that too."

You look at him. You almost want to be mad at him for not feeling guilty about leaving the kids once again this week. I mean, you feel guilty, why doesn't he? You know he's right. Sometimes, it's these date nights that keep you sane. After all, you know you'll have a good time. You always do.

Tip #4–Make a Little "We" Time.

Now, why wouldn't you think that you deserve a date night out just like everyone else? Is it the fact that you've already spent every day this week at work away from your kids, so why would you want to leave them again on the week-end? Yes, it's an understandable guilt that can sometimes be overbearing. Don't forget that your husband needs some of your time, too. Men don't feel that same guilt as working moms. Why is that?

It's so easy to grow apart because there's always somebody else or something else to take care of. Remember what's really important. Take care of yourself, take care of your family, and take the time to take care of your relationship with your husband.

Tip #5–Expect the Unexpected.
Sick Kids

"What do you mean you don't feel good? Let me feel your forehead. Okay, it's a little warm. Now what should we do?" You're sure your son can hear the angry tone in your voice.

You try to remain upbeat. You're thinking, *poor kid*! He's not sick on purpose. You try not to think about the fact that it's the second time this month he's sick and that you'll have to take another day off at work. Won't they be impressed? You know you have more than enough family sick days to cover it, but nevertheless, you still feel like a heel. You feel guilty about not going into work. Then, you also feel a pang of guilt not automatically putting your family first without hesitation. It's not that they're not a priority, you're just doing what you do best, trying to make everyone happy.

This hesitation is a regular part of balancing out your family and work life. You start making plans at six o'clock in the morning. Your mind races. "Okay, if he's not feeling better by 7, I'll call my mother-in-law to see if she can watch him today. (You decide on 7 because you know she should be up by then and that still gives you an hour for a miracle to happen in hopes that he feels better.) If she can watch him, great! Then I won't have to take the day off work today. I could maybe call my husband, but he doesn't get sick days, and he's already gone for the day so that's out of the question. Besides, he makes more money than me, so it's unreasonable to even think that he should stay home. And if my mother-in-law can't watch him, I'll have to fax in my work plans to the office so someone else can cover my appointments. Oh boy, they won't be happy."

As you continue to get yourself ready for the day with hopeful optimism, you know darn well your son won't be able to go to school. And you know that if he can't go to school, the babysitter won't want to watch him either because he'll get everyone else sick.

When seven o'clock rolls around, all hope is not lost. He's not feeling any better, but your mother-in-law is home and available. Whoopee! You would do a happy dance, but that wouldn't look good in front of your sick child who would probably get the wrong impression (then you'd really scar him for life). Okay, today got off to a rough start, but things are looking up.

You're grateful that you have a strong support group to help you out when you need it. Now, if you could just stop thinking about how your sick child is doing all day and stop feeling guilty that you're not the one at home feeding him his chicken soup.

❖

Tip #5–Expect the Unexpected.

There's always going to be something coming up unexpectedly. And face it; you can only be so prepared. It is important to have a strong support system, whether it's your mom, sister, or neighbour down the street. If there are people you can count on to help you through a crisis or your day to day activities, your stress load will be a lot lighter.

Not everyone has a husband who can take a day off work with a sick kid, and not everyone has a mother or mother-in-law who lives 10 minutes away. You have to create a support system that works for you. It could perhaps be trading off childcare with your neighbour, or getting to know the widowed senior across the street who doesn't seem to have much family around and who would perhaps feel needed by helping you out.

Creating a support system is easier said than done, and you don't have to do it on your own. Start talking to your neighbours who may know someone, or maybe even with people at work.

Don't forget that a support system goes both ways, so be prepared to step in and help others also. A give-and-take relationship requires some work, but it is definitely worth it.

Tip #6–Make Lemonade.
Funny Bunny

You mumble and you roll over in bed as you hear the TV blaring in the living room. Argh! It can't be time to get up already. As you roll over, you glance at your alarm clock. Yep, 6:45 on a Sunday morning. You wonder why your kids never seem to sleep in on weekends. Maybe it's a little revenge from the Big Guy upstairs from you doing the same thing to your parents growing up (according to the stories you've heard anyway). Nevertheless, you figure you probably have about eleven minutes of television watching before one of your kids comes wandering in telling you he's hungry.

Eleven wonderful, glorious, peaceful minutes . . . zzz. You barely start to doze off when you quickly bolt up quickly in bed. Crap! It's Easter Sunday. How could you forget? It comes once a year, and yet it still manages to sneak up on you without you noticing. You thought about it yesterday. Why, oh why didn't you write yourself a note? Now, what are you going to do?

You can't even yell at your husband for letting you forget since he's already left for work. Oh, is he ever lucky to be working this morning! Now, you know it's not really his fault that you forgot, but why is the onus always on you for these kinds of things. Why doesn't he do stuff for the holidays once in a while? Oh well, that's an argument for another time. And time is not something you have this morning.

The only thing going for you is the fact that your kids seem to have forgotten also about the Easter Bunny, since they haven't mentioned him yet. It's a good thing you bought their Easter treats last month. At least you have something stashed away in the closet. Now, what to do?

You know you have to get creative.

You quickly bundle up all the Easter treats in one of your bed blankets and tiptoe into the kitchen. You notice that your kids are still in a daze as they stare at the TV. Obviously, they're still in the waking-up process. You manage to bump into two kitchen chairs and trip on a rubber toy in front of the fridge on your way to the front entrance. As quietly as possible, you set up their Easter baskets by the front door and quickly scamper back to the bedroom. The whole process doesn't take more than seven minutes, but it feels like an eternity.

Sure enough, your kids coming looking for you about four minutes later.

"Mom, I'm hungry. Are you getting up?" They whine as they start to make their way into your bed.

"Hey boys, do you know what day it is today?" You try to sound like you just woke up, but your adrenaline is still pumping.

"Yeah, it's Scooby-Doo Sunday and then church, right?"

Bless their souls. "Sure it is, but it's also Easter Sunday. Who comes on Easter Sunday?" You like getting them primed.

"The Easter Bunny!" They start jumping up and down and screaming. Face it: who really needs an alarm clock on Easter Sunday?

"That's right! Did he come last night?"

"No, he didn't. There's nothing in the living room!" Their fallen faces make you want to laugh, but you hold back.

"He must've come last night. Check all over the house. The Easter Bunny sometimes likes to play jokes on kids. Maybe he hid your baskets?" Phew! You manage to cover your ass once again!

They run off yelling and looking all over the house. They are so happy to find their baskets in the front entrance. Actually, you think this was probably more fun having them search for their treats than placing them out on the couch like you usually do.

"Mom, that Easter Bunny is funny. He's a funny bunny, isn't he?" They start laughing through the chocolate on their faces.

Look at that! You may have even created a new tradition in your household this morning. That wasn't your intention, but it's great how things work out!

Tip #6–Make Lemonade.

Sure, things aren't always going to go your way! Should you let it get you down? No way! You should try and make the best of it because you never know how things may turn out in the end.

This, of course, is fairly easy to do if you're a positive thinker. Now, if you're not, it takes a little training. The expression, "It could be worse . . ." can always be used when you're starting to feel sorry for yourself. Face it; there is always somebody out there in a worse situation. So, how can you justify complaining about your problems?

You're only human and it's natural to have a little self-pity every once in a while. But don't forget that your kids are learning from you. Seeing how you handle yourself in difficult situations will impact how they will handle their own problems in the future.

Tip #7–Keep It Simple.
Birthday Parties

You're driving home from work with a hundred thoughts running through your mind all having to do with your son's birthday party tomorrow. You go through the invisible checklist of the things that have to get done. This, of course, is at the same time as you are driving through heavy traffic and listening to your kids fighting in the back seat.

Your son wants a Spiderman theme and you don't want to disappoint him. After all, you don't want him growing up believing his mom didn't care about him because he never had *fun* birthday parties. You feel he's already sacrificed so much because you're a working mom. So, why not give him a party to remember?

While you're frantically vacuuming the house after the kids are in bed and the cake is baking in the oven, you wonder, *why didn't I think of picking up a cake at the store?* You update your husband as to what's planned for the party tomorrow. I mean, heaven forbid the other Moms see your dirty house as they drop off their kid for the party. They probably won't see more than the front entrance, but just in case, you had better do the bathroom, too. And what if they decide to come in for a cup of coffee when the party is over? You'd better do the living room and kitchen. And while you're at it, the bedrooms could also use a good vacuuming. You don't need these kids going home and telling their Moms that you keep a dirty house. They'll think you can't keep a clean household while also holding down a full-time job. How will you sleep at night? (Note the sarcasm.)

Once the house is up to your standards, you ask your husband to help you put together the treat bags and string up the decorations for tomorrow. Last, but not least, there are still presents to wrap and snacks to put together. Phew! By 11 p.m., you're ready for the party. Exhausted, you fall asleep dreaming about what you forgot to do for tomorrow.

Screaming kids, juice spilling, snacks strewn across the kitchen floor, and wrapping paper bits lying around tells you that the party is a great success. All the kids leave with a treat bag and a smile. A few also leave with stained T-shirts, but now you know not to make grape Kool-Aid again. You know you'll have to attack the cake stain in the carpet that someone managed to sneak in there and somehow grind in the rug. And what about the pieces of gift-wrapping paper that a couple of the kids were shoving in the registers? You're once again exhausted by the time everything is picked up, and your kids are falling asleep on the couch. Your husband, which you have to admit was a great help today, is snoring loudly in his chair.

And if your son ever claims that you don't love him because he never gets any fun parties (he never has yet), you can pull out the Spiderman party pictures to prove him wrong. The unwanted stress and the lack of sleep may have taken the fun out of planning the perfect party, but the tired smile on your son's face, along with the thank-you hug at the end of the night, made it all worthwhile. Face it, next year you'll order pizza, buy the pre-packaged treat bags and cake, and book Playland. Hey, you may be a slow learner, but efficient party-planning comes with practice.

Tip #7–Keep It Simple.

Sure, it's nice to give your kids everything they want. It's also nice to have everything done the way you want it. Keeping things simple will alleviate a lot of stress. Keeping things simple doesn't just come easy; it's something you have to learn to do.

It's okay if your kids don't always have homemade cookies in their lunch. It's okay if your house doesn't get vacuumed daily. It's okay to order take-out for supper once in a while. It's okay to keep things simple. Besides, your kids may not remember that you vacuumed the house every day, but they *will* remember how unhappy you seemed from always being stressed out.

Tip #8–He's Old Enough.
How many kids?

For some reason that morning, your bladder wakes you up unexpectedly at precisely 4:23 a.m. And 4:23 a.m. is precisely 23 minutes after your husband's alarm should've gone off. And at precisely 4:23 a.m., you shake your husband awake and tell him he slept in.

Wow, can your man move when he wants to! Within seven minutes flat, he's out the door with his lunch in hand (pre-made by you the night before of course) making a bee-line for his work truck.

In the meantime, your heart is racing like you've just run a marathon and you're not even the one who slept in. Why is that? He's the one who slept in; he's the one who forgot to set his alarm, and you're the one who can't get back to sleep. You glance at the clock and notice it is now 4:39 a.m., which is precisely one hour and fifty-one minutes before your alarm will go off. And your alarm will go off; you know that for sure.

Lying there awake, you try and understand how husbands can get away with what they do? When your husband runs behind, he can get out the door in seven minutes. If you were to forget to set your alarm, there's no damn way you'd ever be able to pull that off with two kids in tow. By the time you wake the kids up, feed them, get them dressed, get their school stuff organized, and get yourself ready while frantically rushing and screaming like a maniac, you figure it would still take you about forty minutes to have everybody out the door–and that's pushing it. It's not like you're going to try it, but it's an interesting concept.

Sometimes, husbands seem to get off easy. And you have proof of that thinking about how your husband behaved last weekend on the night of the big family party. As you attempt to fall back asleep, you try to imagine what you could've done differently the morning before the party. It started when your husband decided to go and do some work outside. You were thinking that it was a great idea since it gave you the chance to get things picked up in the house and kids cleaned up. Well, his work morning led into a work afternoon. And his work afternoon was definitely not all work and no play because you kept seeing his buddies pull in for a beer. It's not that you mind when his buddies pull in for a beer, it's just that your husband is a kind of a social bug. And he has a hard time telling his buddies that he's got other plans lined up, especially when he's hosting his friends. Maybe he doesn't want to be labelled as "whipped," who knows? All you knew that afternoon was that if he didn't come in and get ready soon, you'd be late for the party. It was only when you were busy getting the kids' shoes on and making sure they had a coat and hat that you're husband flew into the house. Real nice! So it was 4:30 before he quickly stripped down and ran for a shower. Meanwhile, you had started the vehicle, loaded the kids up, along with your vegetable tray and salad, and got the door ready to lock up. In the meantime, you hear your husband yelling at you, wondering where his dress shoes are and what shirt he should wear. He's upset that you didn't lay out his outfit on the bed like last time. What he doesn't realize is that last time there was a family party; he was actually working–not socializing. So of course you didn't mind doing it that time, but you reasoned that it was a little different this time. You just won't tell him that. Instead, you tell him you'll wait for him in the truck. By the time he rushes to the vehicle, dressed, unshaven because he didn't have time (yeah right), and out of breath, it's precisely 4:48. Good thing the party is only a few minutes away in town. Note that you have not said one nagging word to him yet.

As you pull into town, your husband decides to make a stop at the liquor store on the way to the party. You're starting to fume. Okay, you didn't yell at him for not helping get the kids ready for the party. You didn't yell at him for getting in the house late. You didn't yell at him for hosting his own little *party* in the shop when he claimed to be working by discussing future shop expansion plans with experienced trades-men (his buddies). When you actually show up late to a party because your husband had to make a booze stop? Yep, that's a little over the top, especially considering your husband always prides himself on being on time and making fun of others who seem to be on a different time schedule. Yep, that really burns your ass. The fuming turns into sizzling as you pull into the party at 5:08. Of course the stop at the liquor store took longer than expected because he ran into an old neighbour.

As you walk into the door, the potluck line has already started and you hurry to get your salad and vegetables on the table. Yes, everybody seems to notice that you're late. What really makes you pop is when your husband casually mentions to one of his uncles the reason you're late for the party. "Yeah, well my wife didn't lay my clothes out like she usually does. That's why we're running late." What. What? What! What in hell was that? Your fault. Your fault? Your fault! Oh, this means war. Oh, he'll hear about it on the way home, at home, and all next week. And he'll probably hear about it before the next few family parties. You know men don't like nagging wives, but they sure don't seem to help their cause with their stupidity sometimes.

Thinking about the events of last weekend, your blood starts to boil again. Great, there's no way you'll be able to get back to sleep now. You glance at the clock and notice that it's precisely 5:46. You might as well get up since you've wasted over an hour in bed. You sit up! Nope, you're not quite ready to do that yet. You continue to toss and turn and the last time you remember looking at the clock, it said precisely 5:58.

At 6:30 your alarm goes off. Boy, now are you tired. It turns out to be a long morning, a long afternoon, and an even longer evening. You're very happy later that evening once the kids are watered, fed, and in bed. You now have a chance to sit down and watch that TV show scheduled for 9:00 you've been waiting a week to see.

By 9:17, you're already starting to nod off. When you finally come to, the clock now indicates that it's precisely 9:48. Great, you've missed the whole show and you're half asleep. Screw the show. You finally decide to give in to what your body's trying to tell you . . . it's time for bed.

By precisely 9:57, you jump into bed and sink into the pillow. You can already feel your eyes droop when your husband decides to join you. Through your heavy lids, you can tell he's got that look in his eye. Oh, no! Not tonight.

What to do? It's easy; you basically blow him off and roll over. You know he's not very happy, and he probably has no idea why you're not interested. Face it; men aren't always great at figuring these things out. It must be some genetic defect or something. You're thinking you want to yell, "It's your fault, you Nincompoop! I'm tired because of you. I'm tired because you forgot to set your alarm. I'm tired because you really peeved me off last weekend. I'm tired and I missed my TV show." Yelling at him would be way too tiring. Then it would probably lead to an hour-long discussion, then to a heated argument, and finish eventually with make-up sex. Sounds like way too much work and then he'd win anyway if there was make-up sex. So you opt for the quicker, less-tiring way out; you roll over and fall asleep. He can hear you snoring in exactly two minutes.

Yes, working mom, kids are tiring, but when you have to look after your husband too, it can double your workload. It might even be your fault for caring a little too much. Besides, he's a big boy! It might be time to give him a little more responsibility!

Tip #8–He's Old Enough.

Yes, that's right, working mom! It's time to split the workload up a little bit. You're so used to taking on a little bit more, and a little bit more, and a little bit more.

Your husband is now old enough to lay out his own clothes and set his own alarm. If he forgets, he'll only do it once. You shouldn't have to take that on, too! You've got enough on your own plate with your own alarm and all the rest that comes with it–like getting the kids up and getting them ready in the morning.

The more independent he is, the more he'll be able to take care of himself. Remember, you're his wife, not his mother.

Tip #9–Learn to Laugh at Yourself.
Cop Stop

You barely hear your son yelling at you from the back seat on your way home from work. You're too distracted by the fifty million thoughts running through your brain. Okay, maybe not fifty million, but a heck of a lot. *What should I make for supper tonight? Hmm, maybe chicken strips and fries; no, Sloppy Joes would be a better choice since I don't have any ketchup left in the fridge. I'd better put ketchup on my grocery list for tomorrow. Now, where did I put that list? It must be on the fridge next to the dry-cleaning stub. Oh yeah, I gotta do that tomorrow, too. Okay, groceries, dry cleaning, and I know there's something else I have to do tomorrow. What was it? Aha! An oil change. Okay, groceries, dry cleaning, oil change . . .   oh, and I can't forget my hair appointment scheduled after work for me and the kids. Shoot, why didn't I write this down at home last night? So, there are four things I have to remember to write down when I get home–no, make that five! I also need to pick up the mail.*

Your son attempts to get your attention once again. You half-heartedly respond as you're still thinking of the list in your head.

"Hmm! What do you need?"

"Mom, look behind you!" He sounds almost desperate.

"Why, what is it?" You're so used to his drama; you assume it's nothing important.

"Look, Mom! That cop's lights are flashing." He's blunt and to the point.

Okay! Now that got your attention. Cops! You glance in your rear-view mirror. Oh crap! He's right; there are cops behind you and . . . oh great; they're trailing you! You slowly pull over and wonder why they're stopping you? As you're pulling over, you realize that you were in a school zone. No wonder everyone else seemed to be driving so slowly tonight.

"Mom, are you going to jail?" Now, if you weren't the one in this situation, you might actually laugh at his comment.

"No, son. I think Mom was driving a little too fast." Your attempt to soothe him doesn't work and you can see the tears start to well up in his eyes.

"Why were you driving too fast? Don't you know how to drive?"

Okay, he nailed you with that comment without even realizing it.

Just then, the officer comes to your window asking for your registration and driver's license. You do as you're told, answer his questions courteously and attempt to explain why you were driving over the speed limit. You wonder if maybe you should fib a little to help your situation. As you glance in your rear-view mirror, you realize that your son probably wouldn't let you get away with it anyway. Just as you're about to answer another one of his questions, your son pipes in.

"Officer, are you going to put my mom in jail until she learns how to drive good?"

Well, the officer gets a kick out of that comment. He enjoys it so much that he lets you off with a warning and tells your son to keep an eye on your driving. Your son is happy to oblige, and he takes his responsibility seriously. So much so that he takes it upon himself to question your driving all the way home and the rest of the week, for that matter. Hey, you're not complaining. After all, he did get you out of a ticket. However, you're wondering if it's worth it since he tells the story to everyone he knows about how his mom got pulled over by the cops. Now, you'll never live it down!

Tip #9–Learn to Laugh at Yourself.

You know nothing is more annoying than someone who can't admit they screwed up. They want to believe that mistakes happen to everyone else, but not them. And they are so ready to point the finger and dish out blame when someone else is at fault. Yet, when something happens to them, there's always an excuse or someone else to take the fall. Face it, all you want to do is give the finger right back at them when that happens (and you know what finger you're thinking about).

Learn to laugh at yourself. Most of the time, people are going to know when you screwed up because someone will tell them (like your son from the back seat) or it'll creep into some kind of conversation sooner or later. Why hide it? You're only human! Besides, once your little secret is out in the open, you'll feel a little lighter since there won't be as much weight on your shoulders.

Don't forget that your kids are always watching to see how you handle yourself in these kinds of situations. They're kind of like little monkeys imitating your every move. So expect them to blame someone else when you ask them who broke your favourite vase if you, yourself, are a blamer. And expect them to admit their mistakes and willingly accept the consequences if you, yourself, are woman enough to own up to your own mistakes.

Tip #10–Get a Fridge Calendar.
Get Organized.

You come from work, pile your stuff up on the kitchen counter and start thinking about what to make for supper. As you walk over to the fridge to take out the milk, you glance at your fridge calendar staring at you in the face. Oh my God, there's an important meeting tonight at 7. How could you have forgotten? You quickly change your supper plans from lasagne to ordering out for pizza. Dishes and homework are done in record time and you decide that the kids could go without baths tonight. You quickly give your husband last-minute instructions before you rush out the door and promise to be back after the meeting and stopping at the store to pick up some groceries on the way home. You check to make sure you have your cell phone on the way out and pray the roads are good.

At the meeting, somebody comments as to how organized you are. She's impressed at how you're able to remember everything amidst your busy work day. You know she's a working mom too. You just smile and shrug your shoulders. Why don't you want her to know your secret? Is it kind of like a competition to see who can do it better– "Women Who Can Survive the Working Mom Syndrome without Letting Other People Know What They're Going Through"? You almost want to tell her your secret because you know she's only been back at work for a couple months. Nah! She'll figure it out on her own eventually.

You love your fridge calendar because it helps make your life a little easier. The hardest thing to do is to get in the habit of remembering to write down important information as soon as you get it (meetings, sports, birthdays, etc.) The key is to have a calendar with big enough squares to allow you to add lots of critical information without overcrowding it. Colour coding works well, too (red for meetings, blue for sporting functions, etc.)

You arrive home after your meeting feeling great about yourself. You don't hear those compliments enough. As you walk to the fridge for a glass of juice to celebrate your personal victory, you hear a POP! That must be the sound of your bubble bursting! As you glance at your fridge calendar once again while shutting the door, you realize what you did. Sure you managed to make the meeting, but you forgot your anniversary last week.

Now the big decision is do you acknowledge to your husband that you forgot your anniversary (he must've too because he obviously never mentioned anything). If you do, he'll always be able to use this against you in the future. Or, do you not mention it at all, pretending you always knew about it, but you were waiting for him to say something first? Either way, you screwed yourself out of a gift or at least an apologetic bouquet of flowers.

Tip #10–Get a Fridge Calendar.

Now, you're probably thinking *why* a fridge calendar? The fridge is something you open up at least twenty times a day, especially with kids. And if you're opening the fridge at least twenty times a day, the calendar is staring at you in the face at least twenty times a day. Therefore, that's twenty more times you'll see that dentist appointment scheduled for Friday at 2. That's twenty more times you'll remember your son's "Show'n Tell" at school. That's twenty more times a day to remind you that you shouldn't forget to call your dad on his birthday.

A fridge calendar is convenient, simple, and very accessible. So why make your life more complicated? There's also the option of using different colour codes for different important events. For example, sports are written in blue, appointments are written in red, birthdays are in black, and so forth. You have to figure out a system that works for you. And then, train your partner and kids to do the same.

Life's complicated enough already; why not keep it simple with a little organization?

Tip #11–S@&! Happens.
Shopping Scare

"Where are you? Come out right now." You're sure your harsh whisper can be heard by everyone in the store. You hear no response.

"Come out now; I mean it." Your whisper gets a little bit louder. Still nothing.

"Okay, you think you're funny. I'm not laughing. There's going to be trouble if you don't come out right now." You can start to hear the desperation in your voice.

Where is he? He was here two seconds ago. You know he snuck under one of the clothing racks, but which one? You're thinking *why did this happen to me*? You're tired; you know he's tired, and the baby is sound asleep in the stroller. Boy, what rotten luck!

All you wanted to do was pick up a birthday gift for the party you were taking your kids to this coming weekend. And, of course, today after work was the only time you had to do it. Why, oh why, do things have to get so complicated? A 10 minute shopping trip is already turning into 20 minutes, you still haven't found a gift, and your son decides to play hide-and-seek in the clothing racks. You promise yourself that if you can get through today, you'll be smarter about these shopping trips! Next time, either you'll go after the kids are in bed or you'll put money in a card. Why didn't you just do the money thing? You know it's not as personal, but it sure would've saved you this hassle.

Now the staff is giving you a hand looking underneath all of the racks in the search for your son. The next few minutes feel likes hours and you begin to panic. Where is he? You know he couldn't have left the store because you're standing right beside the front entrance. *Okay, breathe* you tell yourself, *and try a different approach.*

"If you come out, we'll get you some ice cream." You hope people don't judge your desperate parenting methods. Still nothing.

After a couple of minutes, one of the clerks calls your over to a clothing rack of winter coats. You see your son snuggled up on one that must have fallen onto the floor underneath the others. He's snoring softly and drool is pooling under his chin. He looks like an angel and for a second, and only a split second, you forget why you're mad. Then it comes back to you. What can you do? He's safe and sound and once he wakes up, he probably won't even remember what he did.

So, after thanking the sales staff a thousand times, you manage to carry your sleeping son, while pushing the stroller out to the car. You leave without buying anything and when you get home, you realize you still don't have a birthday gift. You manage to find a birthday card and you seal it up with some money in it. You decide it's not worth going back to the store again. From that moment on, you start stock-piling gifts. In other words, you always have a few on hand to choose from should an unexpected birthday party come up. Since then, you feel a little more prepared and your blood pressure gets a break from the nerve-wrenching shopping trips.

Tip #11–S@&! Happens.

Sometimes s*@! happens! The only thing you can do is learn from these unexpected circumstances! Is this the first time stuff like this has happened? No. Will this be the last time? Unfortunately, no. Will you do some things differently from now on? Of course.

Well then, what else can you ask for? No one was hurt or lost. And you, of course, learned to change the way you do things. For example, pre-buying birthday gifts is a good idea. And sending money in a card is perhaps a great idea (maybe not very personal, but practical).

Sure it sucks when these things happen! Hey, you're only human. Besides, what are they going to do, fire you from being a parent? At least you know that job is secure!

Tip #12–Take What You Can Get.
Your 15 Minutes

You gotta love that feeling of crashing on the couch after a long week's work. Ahhh...Friday night! Your head finds that couch cushion fairly easily, and your eyes seem to droop ever so slowly until you hear yourself snore. It's weird. The fact that you can actually hear yourself snore is strange enough. That your own snoring doesn't even seem to bother you? Whatever, it's too much to think about right now.

You know you're relaxed because your kids are quiet and they really seem to be enthralled by whatever's on TV. And you don't even care what they're watching. Okay, it's not that you don't care; it's that you just don't have the energy right now. Earlier, you did glance at the TV to make sure it was a cartoon your kids were watching before you hit the couch. And you know that *Family Guy* or *Futurama* isn't on before supper. Phew, you're safe! You chuckle to yourself thinking back that your mom must have done the same with you and your choice of television programming. Except it wasn't *Family Guy* she was worried about; it was *The Simpsons*. Boy oh boy, have we come a long way! Not in a good way, perhaps, but nevertheless, things seem to progress or regress as far as TV shows.

From experience, you know that you have about fifteen to twenty minutes before one of your kids needs something like a snack or a glass of water. So, when your youngest wakes you up exactly seventeen minutes later, you're not surprised, just a little disgusted.

"Hey, Mom! Wake up!" Why is it children don't understand how to whisper, especially your children?

"Huh? What?" You mumble as your hand automatically reaches to clear the drool from your chin. (That's always a sign of a great nap.)

He starts shaking you awake with such vigour. "Mom! Mom! Look! Look!"

"Huh? What is that?" You slowly open your eyes to a finger being shoved in your face. You cross your tired eyes, while trying to focus on his finger shoved in front of your nose.

"Look at that? Isn't that the biggest booger? I need a Kleenex." Oh yum! He always has a great way in suppressing your appetite before supper. It's kind of a mystery as to why you still can't fit into your pre-baby clothes. You've skipped way more meals because of him, and yet the weight still hangs in there (literally)!

"Oh yuck! Get a Kleenex. You can do it yourself. You're big enough!"

"No, I can't. There's no more in the box. You have to get me one!" He starts whining, while swinging his "booger" finger around the room.

You figure it's time to get off the couch! You know you probably only have a couple of minutes before he starts scaring his brother with it. Then you know the fight will be on.

You groggily fumble through the hall closet trying to find the boxes of Kleenex. No luck! You thought for sure you had another one left. Oh yeah! You remember that you opened it yesterday to replenish the empty box in the bathroom. So, you make your way to the bathroom and rush to grab one from there.

You're two minutes too late. You can hear screaming coming from the living room. You know exactly what's going on, and their yelling confirms it.

"Get that booger away from me! You're disgusting!" Sure, the older, more mature one is upset with his younger brother. You figure he's probably more upset with the fact that he didn't think of this little booger trick in the first place.

You make your way back into the living room screaming at the kids as you go. Nothing wakes you up more from your comfortable snooze then a good scream (note the sarcasm).

You split them up, calm them down, threaten to change the channel ...you know, the usual. When they seem to calm down in their separate chairs, you offer the Kleenex to your youngest.

"No thanks, Mom. I don't need it!"

"What do you mean you don't need it? You woke me up for this!" Do they have to hit every nerve today?

"No, I don't need it anymore. I wiped it on the couch. See?" Oh, you've got to be kidding. You just had your furniture cleaned last week. Yep, there it is. He must've really taken the time to ground in the big green and yellow booger staring at you from the centre cushion of the couch.

After scolding him, sending him to his room, yelling at his brother for laughing at him, and cleaning up the smeared mess, you're ready for another snooze. Now is not the time; you've got to get supper started.

Your fifteen minutes is up anyway. People wish for their fifteen minutes of fame. You're just happy with getting fifteen minutes-no make that seventeen minutes-of quiet time.

Until next week ...

Tip #12-Take What You Can Get.

When you think about it, you should be happy you had fifteen minutes to yourself on the couch. These moments happen so few and far between that you must savour and appreciate them.

Now, why is it that you seem to pay dearly for that precious time after it's come and gone? Who knows, but take what you can get. Some other Moms can only wish for those fifteen or seventeen minutes on the couch. You're very lucky! Okay, maybe not when it comes time to boogers, but it'll give you something to talk about at your son's wedding in about twenty years. Yes, revenge is sweet, but sometimes slow.

Tip #13–Love Yourself.
Looking in the Mirror

Every now and then, you have a chance to check yourself out in the full-length mirror in your underwear. Yes, you'd like to check yourself out naked, but it's too much of a risk with the kids around. And then the questions will start and you're not ready for that. No, you're better off keeping your clothes on.

So after studying yourself for a minute or so, you think *Wow* (and not in a good way)! Maybe if you take two steps back, it'll take off five pounds? And so you try it and think, *Yeah, that's better.* You keep going. Maybe if you squint your eyes, your love handles will magically disappear. And by sucking in your cheeks, you'll look at least three years younger. And if you raise your eyebrows, your wrinkles will fade. Heck, realistically, if you just get dressed, it'll hide most of your problem areas.

You know your body is the result of the work you put into it. That extra twenty pounds isn't going to come off without your effort. You have to spend time to work it off, but the hard part is finding the time. Where does it go? You could wake up an extra half hour in the morning before the kids do. Of course, you've tried it before and what usually happens is that the kids hear you dancing and grunting and end up getting up earlier too. You could also do it during your lunch hour. Then again, the other errands you usually run wouldn't get done until after work. So that won't work. There's always a little time after the kids are in bed. Who really feels like doing it then? You continue to justify your excuses. Face it; you have to make the time and you're not ready to . . . just yet. Maybe next week? Yeah, next week sounds better. You're so focussed on your thoughts that you barely hear your son wander in. This confirms your decision in keeping your clothes on.

"Mom, what are you doing?" You leave kids alone for five minutes and they have to come and find you. Why is that?

"What do you mean?" You answer as you continue checking yourself out in the mirror.

"Why do you look like a surprised fish?"

Well, that gets your attention. You burst out laughing, and he does too. The difference is he doesn't know why? It's now obvious to you that sucking in your cheeks and raising your eyebrows aren't helping your cause. It's probably a good thing your little "reality check" walked in.

"So I look like a surprised fish, hey?" You ask him as you start tickling him as a way of showing your appreciation for his honesty. After a couple of minutes, you both end up falling on your bed, exhausted from laughing.

"Mom, why were you doing that in the mirror?" You know his curiosity won't be satisfied until you tell him what you were doing. Face it; he gets that gene from your side of the family.

"Well, sometimes Mommy likes to try different things to make herself look better." You try the truth. Isn't it supposed to set you free?

"Why do you need to look better? I love you already." Spoken like a true angel, your true angel. Sometimes, that's really all we need to hear. It's sometimes easy to forget that even though we're often short on time, we're never short on love.

Tip #13–Love Yourself.

(There's nothing dirty about this suggestion, but hey, take it like you want, it's whatever works for you). Eating healthier and exercising regularly will make you feel better. And the extra energy does come in handy being a working mom. Face it; no one else can do it for you. Looking after yourself is another one of your many jobs.

You are what you make of yourself. Yes, time is not always on your side, and we all know it takes time to look good. And of course, taking more time to yourself means having less time for your family. The merry-go-round of guilt is a vicious cycle.

A happy mom means a happy family, right? And so, the extra personal time is justified (at least you try and convince yourself).

Tip #14–A Little "Me" Time
Shopping With the Girls

Today's a day of freedom! Well, for the most part. You finally decide to take your friends up on their offer to go shopping for the day. It was a tough decision, but you figure you'll go since you have a lot of birthdays you need to buy gifts for anyway. Not that you really need to go out of the house to actually shop these days (there's catalogues and a computer with the Internet at home), but it's your justification in making you feel a little less guilty about going along and leaving the kids at home with their dad. Besides, your friends don't seem to mind leaving their kids behind.

Mind you, the kids might not necessarily be *at home* with their dad when you're gone. What will probably happen is he'll call his mom to see if she's home. He'll either end up dropping the kids off there for a good part of the day because he absolutely has to do something, and he can't take the kids with him (even if it's his day off). She'll feed them, change them, and probably end up bathing them before they actually do end up back at home. You won't find out about this arrangement until you actually get home, which is probably a good thing; otherwise, you would've decided not to go out shopping at all.

You know that this shopping trip has to be productive. You make grocery lists, gift lists for the birthdays coming up, lists of clothing needs for the kids, and you also take your husband's list. His thought is, since you're going into the city anyway, you can pick up some things for him. You're a little overwhelmed at how many places you have to stop and how many things you have to buy, but you're optimistic that there will be no lines, traffic, or any other hold-ups. You have offered to drive, because you figure this way you can stop where you want and make sure you get everything you need.

The day starts off pretty good when you realize everyone wants to stop at the same stores as you (they must all have husbands too). Too bad the line-ups at some of these places chew up a lot of your time. It's especially frustrating when you try to find someone at the hardware store to try and help you find that wax bowl ring for the toilet, which is at the top of your husband's list. First off, you have no clue as to what it's for or what it looks like. You just know that your husband needs it for the bathroom renovations you've been after him to finish. You've been waiting for him to finish these renovations for about a month, and you're not leaving the store without it.

The first store employee you find happens to have just started her job that day and she is not quite sure where to find it but is willing to look with you. (It takes 10 minutes of searching with her before convincing her to get someone else to help.) To top it all off, in this day of technology, your husband conveniently doesn't have his cell phone with him and you can't get hold of him to get a description of this ring. Great! You stop and take a breather to try and convince yourself that shopping is fun as you continue to look for the next three items on your husband's list.

Overall, you manage to have a pretty good day with the girls and you take a few moments to close your eyes during your lunch to listen and enjoy the adult conversation at your table. There's no yelling, screaming, tugging on your pants, spilling, or burping. You do kind of chuckle to yourself afterward because although you enjoyed it, most of the lunch conversation was based on who you left behind for the day!

When you get home, your husband helps you unload your purchases and takes a look at some of the stuff you bought. He asks you how much you spent that day and is appalled by how much you actually admit to. When you look at your receipts, you look at how much you spent on groceries, the kids, the stuff he wanted, gifts, and then you realize you did not buy one thing for yourself.

Great! You really needed a couple of new sweaters for work. Oh well, you'll just add them to the next shopping trip, which will probably be in about six months–just in time for Christmas. In the meantime, your old sweaters will have to do.

❖

Tip #14–A Little "Me" Time

No, a little "me" won't turn your kids against you; neither will it make you a bad mother. This "me" time kind of works with the "love your-self" tip mentioned earlier. Loving yourself is also having some time to yourself, however you want to spend it and with whom you want to spend it with.

Your kids have friends, your husband has friends; don't you think you're entitled to having friends of your own? Sure, maybe you started associating with most of your friends because you had something in common. That *something* usually is having kids the same age or husbands that get along. Face it, how many friends do you associate with if their husbands and your husband don't get along? Now, hold on! Don't get your panties in a knot thinking *Yeah, how fair is that?* because it probably works the other way around, too. It's probably a rare thing for you to hang out with wives you can't stand or have nothing in common with because your husbands are friends. And if you do, stop! It'll make your life easier.

A little "me" time is not a bad thing although the guilt might make it feel that way. The key is balance, although it can be hard to achieve.

Tip #15–Change It Up!
Babies and Bellies

Sometimes the most memorable conversations occur at the most unexpected times.

It's a beautiful autumn day as you drive your eldest to school that morning. His art project was too big to bring with him on the bus this morning. You're so busy admiring the crisp frost on the ground that you fail to notice your son's nose wrinkling in thought. This usually means you're in for a good discussion.

He casually asks, "Mom, where do babies come from?"

Whoa! You're wondering where this question came from? You keep your eyes on the road at hand and avoid all eye contact with the questioning baby blues that are staring at you from your right. Face it; so far you've been lucky enough to avoid this question, but the inevitable is the inevitable. It's actually too bad since the morning was off to such a great start. And how come these questions never seem to come up when their father's around? You take your time thinking of how to approach this topic cautiously.

"Well son, it starts out when two people love each other . . ."

He interrupts your well-thought-out start with, "Yeah, yeah, yeah Mom. I mean how does the baby come out?"

Okay! So he doesn't want the "how-the-baby-is-made" details, but rather the "how-the-baby comes-out" details. Hmmm, this could be easier than you thought.

You blurt out, "From the belly button." What in hell made you say that, you chicken? Really? The belly button! The belly button?

"Oh, okay." You can see his mind racing as he's trying to figure out how that would actually work. He is a math kid, that's for sure.

After a few intense seconds of thinking, he continues, "The belly button, really? Well then, how does it come out of the belly button?"

Great! Now you really got yourself in a pickle (actually the whole baby story involves a pickle, but now is not the time to think about that). "Well, the belly button stretches." You keep your answers short and to the point. No sense in giving him more to question.

"Wow! It stretches that big. Boy, no wonder your belly looks like that after you had us?"

"What do you mean . . . looks like that?" You're wondering what he's talking about?

"Well, it kind of looks like a mushy donut. That must be from all the stretching."

You casually glance down at your frumpy middle pushing up against the blouse you thought was so cute this morning. Time to retire it after today.

He starts retracting his comments, realizing what he said wasn't very nice.

"I mean, you look good, Mom." He sits back and smiles.

He thinks that's all it's going to take to make up for that comment. Oh well, considering he's about one-fifth your age, you decide it's best just to let it go.

"So Mom, does it just stretch and the baby comes out and that's all? Is that how I was born?" Oh boy! He's obviously not satisfied with the responses he's been getting so far.

"Sure, that's about it." No sense mentioning the months of back-aches, nausea, and weight-gain leading up to it. And of course, there's also no sense in mentioning the contractions, ambulance ride, pain medication, forceps, or stitches involved in his birth. You'll save those titbits of information for when you really want him to feel guilty, like maybe during his teenage years. Besides, it may just open up another can of worms.

"Oh, okay. Hey, Mom, can we go to the park after school?"

Phew! He's onto a different topic. You're safe, for now. "We'll see..." you mutter as you pull into the school parking lot after what seemed like an ever-lasting morning ride.

He gives you a kiss good-bye before he jumps out of the vehicle with his art project in his arms. You're silently grateful that he's still young enough to give you a kiss good-bye and young enough to still accept your explanations without question. As you pull away, you can hear him whistling as he walks into the school. You remind yourself that you'd better mention this conversation to your husband tonight so that you're both on the same page for next time.

You have to admit, life is never boring. What's next month, Santa?

Tip #15–Change It Up!

That memorable conversation would've never existed if you wouldn't have driven to school that day. That memorable conversation will stick with you for the rest of your life, and maybe even his. Eventually, you'll be able to laugh about it.

Notice, I said *eventually*, not tomorrow.

Yes, routines are necessary, working mom. Sometimes, changing it up leads to unexpected treasures that are just as important.

Tip #16–Set Realistic Goals.
New Year's Blues

It's already March and you think back to the unrealistic, frustrating New Year's resolutions you set for yourself earlier in the year.

First of all, you wanted to push yourself to read more, like maybe a novel a month. Sure, it seemed reasonable. It never used to take you any time to read a novel from cover to cover. Although, that was before kids when you had a little more time on your plate and a little more energy in the evening. You remember that sometimes you couldn't even put the book down until it was finished. Now, it seems like it takes a little too much effort, especially after you've had a long day. Your tired eyes just won't cooperate.

Secondly, you hoped to lose at least twenty pounds. Sure, twenty pounds doesn't seem like much, but it's sure a lot easier and a lot more fun to put on than it is trying to work it off. Admittedly, you've had jeans sitting in your closet for the past five years in hopes of one day getting back into them. It's funny what motherhood does to you. Although you're a lot busier, it's as if your metabolism rebels. Understandably, your body shape won't go back exactly as it was before kids, but it seems to change with every pregnancy. And so, the jeans that fit you in-between having your first two kids won't even make it past your hips after your second. Why is that? The scale tells you your weight is the same, and yet nothing fits properly. It's kind of like the Eighth Wonder of the World. It's no wonder women's clothing companies make so much money. So really, maybe women shouldn't be blamed for wanting to update their wardrobe regularly, because it's actually Mother Nature working her magic (maybe she's a clothes fanatic too).

Lastly, you thought you should learn a new hobby. Sewing has always interested you and you thought maybe you've have a little more time to try something new. And you have no excuse, since your husband bought you the exact, expensive model you wanted for Christmas. You realize that you probably should've done a little more research before diving into this idea. With just the start-up costs, the material costs, learning the machine, pattern searches, and finding space to work, your dream of learning to sew was probably a "brain fart." You may want to attempt it in about fifteen years when the kids are a little older. Really, who are you going to sew for then?

Okay, you look down at the five extra pounds you put on since making these resolutions, and you're disgusted with yourself. Then, you hear the stack of trash magazines you bought this month fall off the counter as your son reaches for a cookie from the cookie jar. Do they count as actual reading material?) You pick up the magazines off the floor and throw them on the new sewing machine (still in the plastic cover) you wanted so badly for Christmas. You've discovered it works great as a coat rack. The guilt of not getting to the sewing machine makes you reach into the cookie jar yourself. Did you say five pounds? You'd better add one more.

Tip #16–Set Realistic Goals.

Why do you do this to yourself? You should be setting realistic goals like counting to 10 before yelling at the kids (okay, at least 8), leaving the house five minutes sooner for work, and maybe trying to find a new deodorant that doesn't cause white flakes. These goals may seem small, but once accomplished, will make you feel a little better about yourself because you've actually reached them. Do you know how happy you'll be when you find that new deodorant?

Tip #17–Don't Take It Personally.
Say What?

Why are kids so honest? No, scratch that. Why are kids so honest at the most inappropriate and unexpected moments? Do they just come by it naturally, or is it something they are prone to do just because they want to piss you off?

You know you love your kids, but you don't always love what comes out of their mouths. It also kind of makes you wonder if they're actually doing it for attention because they feel a little neglected by you, working mom. Maybe you're really just not giving them enough attention at home. Sure, you try and do what you can, but the hours in the day that you spend at home with them are limited. Face it, a working mom's life is always a continual juggling act to try and keep everyone happy. If you're lucky, you may even be happy with yourself.

This is why you always think twice about taking your kids with you to the mall. There is such a variety of people varying in colour, style, and age that it's inevitable that you're going to run into someone different–really different–by the end of the day. So when your sister invites you and the kids to join her at the mall on a Saturday afternoon, you hesitantly agree, crossing your fingers for good measure. Besides, your kids really need new winter boots.

As soon as you arrive at the mall and meet your sister in the front entrance, your stomach flops a little. You know you're in for a wild afternoon. There are people everywhere. Figuring there's still six weeks before Christmas, you thought today would've been a good day to shop before the seasonal rush. Think again! Oh well, you're here already, your sister's here already, and your kids are well rested and restrained in a shopping cart. Let the shopping begin!

The first couple of hours pass by uneventful, but productive considering you managed to find winter boots, winter coats, and a couple of Christmas gifts. Your kids aren't whining yet, but it must be due to the fact that you stopped for ice cream a few minutes earlier. It only took buying one extra cone because your oldest dropped his while walking away from the booth. Thankfully, your youngest never dropped his, but he is disgustingly filthy since his ice cream melted all down the front of his shirt. You're quite sure his shirt saw more ice cream than his mouth. Oh well, that's why they invented baby wipes. It's just too bad you didn't think to bring any.

About ten minutes after finishing the ice cream cones, the sugar rush seems to kick in. It's as if somebody turned a switch on inside your kids. All of a sudden, they seem to really perk up and start talking about everything and to anybody in sight. Your sister thinks it's hilarious, but then again she doesn't have any kids of her own yet to embarrass her. Her time will come.

Pushing the cart down an aisle in a department store (the last stop of the afternoon) proved to be a daunting task. Because the store must've decided to try and put out some Christmas stock that day, everyone was trying to avoid running into things and people as they shopped. Really, putting stock out on a Saturday? Who does that?

Anyway, there's a continual flow of people trying to get by you. One woman even tries to step sideways, attempting to give you a little more room for your shopping cart. And because she's side-stepping, and the fact she's a fairly large woman, her behind barely misses skimming your cart. Bless her soul for not only trying to give you more room, but because of what your son says next.

"Hey, Mom, look at that big butt!" Why is it kids only have one volume–loud—and sometimes even really loud like in this case.

Oh, my God, what to do? What to do? That poor woman never even turns around; she just keeps on walking. After having about two seconds to think about it, you do what mothers do best: ignore and distract. You ignore his remark all together, basically pretending you didn't hear it. Now, this parenting method could backfire if your son decides to repeat his comment louder, thinking you didn't hear him the first time. It's a chance you take, but today is your lucky day, since he doesn't repeat it and you move into the next phase, which is distraction. You quickly draw his attention to a bright new toy displayed on the shelf. It works, and he is enthralled with the new toy for a few minutes. This gives you time to catch your breath and allows your heart to fall back into place. When the woman is clearly nowhere to be seen, you have the big "If you can't say anything nice, than don't say anything at all" talk. You can tell he understands and it sinks in when his eyes start to tear up with regret. Good, that's done! Now, enough shopping; it's time to get home.

Your sister can tell you're a little on edge from what happened today. As you unload your purchases in the back of your vehicle, she tries to make you feel better by saying, "It's true, you know."

"What's true?" You're not sure what she's talking about. You continue to load up your packages.

"About her butt; it was big. He was just stating the obvious." You kind of smirk. Yes, you know it's true, but why does it have to be your son to state the obvious?

Tip #17–Don't Take It Personally.

Sometimes kids will say something for attention purposes; some-times they're just stating the obvious. You can't go blaming it on the fact that you're a working mom, because whether you are working or not, they will say it anyway. And holing your kids up in the house won't work either. It'll drive you nuts, and they'll just have something more outrageous to say when they get out.

Yes, working mom, kids will be kids. They'll drive you nuts.

Tip #18–Appreciate the Little Things.
Picture Day

"Mom, my hair isn't staying down."

"Mom, I spilled milk on my shirt."

"Mom, does this smile look good?"

Ahh! Picture day is here again. You get up extra early to get the kids ready for school. The hair, the outfit, the smile; it's all part of the package. You want your kids to look their best. And so, they leave the house looking like angels. You decide that extra hour in the morning is worth it. You don't want them growing up and looking back at their pictures, thinking that their mom didn't care about how they looked. Or even worse, that you didn't have time to care about how they looked. What would people say if they saw your kids looking shabby on picture day? They wouldn't care that you work full time. That excuse wouldn't be good enough. And so, you do what you can to make things work even if it means losing a little sleep. You leave for work feeling proud of what you accomplished that morning, and you're confidant that it will shine through in their pictures along with their smile.

A few weeks later, the pictures come home from school in their backpacks. It's the same thing every year, and yet you wonder why you're still surprised when you check them out. The fluffed hair is flattened, the pressed shirt is now wrinkled, and you see a small, but noticeable stain. And what is up with that fake, toothy smile? You then smile to yourself because they still look like your angels, and you expected nothing less. Hey, why sweat the small stuff? If they ask about it when they're older, you can always say their dad helped them get ready that morning.

Tip #18–Appreciate the Little Things.

You have to appreciate these precious times in your kids' lives. They are young only once.

Appreciate that your kids are young and full of life. Appreciate that you have a job that pays the bills. Appreciate your health and your family's health. Appreciate your family and friends that are always willing to help out.

You'll often hear a Mom say, "I can't wait until the baby learns to crawl. It'll be so much easier because she'll get around on her own."

When the baby learns to crawl, you hear, "I can't wait until the baby learns to walk; then she won't get as dirty."

When the baby learns to walk, you hear, "I can't wait until she starts school; then I won't have to worry about babysitting."

When she starts school, you hear, "I can't wait until she's older and can stay on her own at home."

When she gets older, you hear, "I can't wait until she's past that teenage stage; then we won't worry as much."

When she's past that teenage stage, you hear, "I can't believe she's moving out already. I can still remember when we brought her home from the hospital. Boy, those were the good ole days."

Appreciate every stage of your children's lives because they grow up so fast. And of course, the older they get, the older you get. And why would you want to wish your life away?

Tip #19–Balance Is Key.
Winding Down

"Why don't you want to watch this one-hour drama with me? Why do you always like to watch the half-hour sitcoms?"

You often hear this question from your husband as you both try and wind down from your workday. You always seem to have the same answer.

"Because, I don't want to think. I want to just sit here and laugh." Face it, who wants to think when you've been thinking all day. Sitting like a zombie in front of the TV for an hour before bed is sometimes just what the doctor ordered. At least, what the doctor should order. After finally cleaning up supper dishes, making lunches, picking up the house, giving the kids' baths, helping them with their homework, tucking them in; you're ready for a little bit of self-meditation in front of the TV. Enjoying the mindless banter on screen and thinking of nothing else seems to really help you really relax. Or maybe it's those three glasses of wine you had at supper. (Yeah right, you only wish!)

As you and your husband decide it's time to hit the hay, your mind starts racing one more time. *Did I set my alarm? Did I sign my son's homework when he showed me he finished it? Did I put all of the lunches back in the fridge? Did I make a note to buy more milk tomorrow? What about eggs and cheese? Might as well buy more yogurt, too. Did I throw that load of laundry in the dryer? Oh no, even that sweater that I'm supposed to let air-dry? Darn, I really liked that sweater. Maybe I can try and stretch it out. Oh well, I guess it was getting kind of old and ratty anyway. Oh, and I can't forget to call the dentist tomorrow. I've been putting that off for too long. And if I'm calling the dentist, I might as well call the optometrist so that I can get the kids done all on the same day if possible. That way, I only miss one day of work instead of two. I'd better not make the appointments for this month since my work schedule is all booked up. Maybe I should make it for next month. Oh, but I wanted to register the kids in swimming lessons then. I know, I'll try to book them in-between our ski weekend at the beginning of next month and swimming lessons.* Yep, that's a plan. Now, what else did I forget to do . . . zzzzzzz? You doze off amidst your deep thoughts of the evening and end up dreaming of trying to stretch your shrunken sweater from the dryer while talking on the phone with your dentist's assistant. Man, you really have to get a life.

You figure that's what these dreams are trying to tell you. This is your life, working mom; this is your life. You know you love your life most days, but you just wish your mind could take a break ever now and then. You decide you really must learn to like wine. Hey, at least you still have your sense of humour!

Tip #19–Balance Is Key.

Burning yourself out is not an option. There are way too many people depending on you. So it's important that you learn to relax. It's an easy word to say, but not so easy to do. It may take some time and practice to try and find something that will help you learn to relax whether it's television, a good book, music, a bath, or even something a little naughtier.

Nevertheless, once you find it, it will make you a more rested, happier, working mom. And how does that saying go? Oh yeah, "When Mom's happy; everyone is happy!"

Tip #20–White Lie, What Lie?
Do What You Gotta Do.

Your son brings home a health homework assignment for the weekend. His teacher wants him to complete a questionnaire on his life to date. After glancing over the questionnaire after supper, you gulp in hesitation. These aren't questions that you expected. You tell your son that there isn't enough time to work on it tonight, but that you'll help him with it, first thing in the morning.

As soon as you kiss the kids goodnight, you bring out their baby books and boxes of pictures and plunk them on the table. Yes, boxes of pictures, not albums. They haven't made their way to albums yet. Your husband wonders in the kitchen and questions what you're up to.

You explain that you've never had time to complete the kids' baby books or organize their pictures properly in the past years. Okay, maybe never had time should actually be you never made time. Face it, you've never missed an episode of your favourite show on TV, but preserving your kids' memories obviously was not a priority. You always knew you'd get to them, you just didn't think you'd be trying to get through them all in one evening.

"Why the heck are you doing this tonight?" He's baffled. He knows how tired you get on Friday nights. And not because his intuition is great, but because you're usually snoring in your favourite chair after the kids are in bed.

"He has to do that health assignment tomorrow. It asks the kids to try and find the answers to the questions themselves by looking through their own baby book first and then asking their parents for help if they need it. The problem is, their baby books aren't even half finished. Actually, not even a quarter filled out. I threw everything in a box because I knew that I would get to it eventually. Just didn't think I'd need to finish all of one in one night." You actually kind of start getting choked up. What kind of mother neglects these things? Oh, you know the answer to that one, working mom.

He actually sits down at the table and starts helping you sift through pictures. Wow, there's a first time for everything. You so badly want to say something, but instead opt to keep your big mouth shut because you really need the help.

Slowly, but surely you manage to find enough pictures to fill up your son's baby book. You find pictures from his previous birthdays. Those were fairly easy to figure out since all you had to do was count the candles on the cake. Yes, you know you're supposed to remember every precious moment in your kids' lives, but face it; there are too many precious moments and too many kids. You also manage to find pictures of his first holiday, his first Christmas, and his first haircut. Okay, Operation Pictures is complete!

Now, onto the first lock of hair. Crap! You know you kept that chunk from the hairdresser, but where oh where, did you put it? Jewellery box? Sock drawer? Closet? No, no, no. Oh well, desperate times calls for desperate measures. You cut off a small chunk of your own hair and shove it into an envelope. Okay, that's done. When you actually find his, you'll replace yours with his. Hey, desperate times call for desperate measures.

Next, you notice that most of his baby weights and heights are vacant. You guess at most of them and do the exact same thing on the empty page that asks you to fill in when all his teeth came in. Which mother actually knows when each of their kids' molars pushed through? And which kid actually let their mother put her finger in their mouth to find out? Really, it's a little ridiculous.

You're happy to see that at least you had already taken the time to fill in the pre-birth information–like the family tree and information about Mom and Dad.

Last, but not least, the footprint page. You know, the one you always dreaded doing. Actually, *dreaded doing* isn't really accurate since you never got to it. After thinking about it, you try an old trick from elementary school. By closing your hand and inking the bottom part of your fist, you carefully stamp the baby book to create the soul of the foot. You then proceed to use your inked fingertips to create the toe prints by lightly touching the page above the marked soul. Not bad at all! You use your other hand to make the other foot. You're proud to say that the second one turned out even better than the first. Okay, you won't actually *say* what you did, since you're not actually proud of what you did either!

After adding a few cute comments to the pictures in the book, you close the book with a sigh. You don't really know if you're sighing because you're happy it's done, or if you're sighing because you're a little disgusted with yourself. It's probably more the latter.

Nevertheless, your son is thrilled while working on his health assignment the next morning. He finishes in record time and you find yourself enjoying watching him find out all about himself. He would've been done even sooner, but you kept thinking about stories to tell him about the pictures in front of him.

You discover you really do remember your son as a baby! You also discover that maybe you're not really the worst mother in the world either. Sure, there's always room for improvement; you can't deny that, that's for sure!

Tip #20–White Lie, What Lie?

It's probably a moral debate to determine if messing with your son's baby book was actually the right thing to do.

On one hand, if you had admitted to him upfront that you never filled in his baby book; he would've felt a little dejected. There would've been tears, whining, and the worst dreaded sentence every Mom despises hearing would've spilled out, "You were the only Mom who didn't do it."

On the other hand, by filling in the baby book the night before and fudging a little of the material, you become the bad guy. And you, as the bad guy, get the pleasure of holding onto that guilt for the rest of your life.

Of course you know that these circumstances were easily avoidable, but you have to face your wrongdoing, working mom. Oh well, what's a little more guilt on your shoulders. If your son ever ends up in therapy, you know that somehow that's going to be blamed on you too.

Tip #21–Enough Guilt Already.
Jealous Much?

You cradle the phone in between your chin and neck as you continue to try and sound enthusiastic about what your cousin has to say about her yoga class. You phoned her to find out if she was coming out to the family reunion and somehow ended up talking about her awesome yoga class.

It's not that you don't care what she has to say, but face it; yoga is not your cup of tea. No, actually, that's putting it mildly. You would rather be stranded on a deserted island without water. You don't care what positions are essential to proper yoga, how important breathing is, or how good she feels afterward. Come on, you've been in labour. You already know what positions are essential and how important breathing is. And the only time you feel great about exercise is after you and your husband . . . ah, well, you know. Okay, maybe you're a little bitter.

What would really interest you is having the time to actually go to a class (it wouldn't even have to be yoga, anyone would do) without finding a babysitting, carrying a car seat, or feeling guilty about having a little free time. So, when you think about it, maybe you're actually a little jealous. Your husband enjoys going out with his buddies at the drop of a hat, why shouldn't you? And you have to admit that he does encourage you to get out sometimes. Although he might consider buying groceries and stopping for the mail "getting out," Who plans the childcare and takes care of the scheduling when you're gone? Oh, that's right; you're expected to do all that too. Really, by the time you weigh the pros and cons of going out for an hour, it's usually not worth leaving the house 45 minutes early to bring the kids to the sitter's, which in turn you have to find yourself, and then rush to pick them up afterward. Thus, a one-hour outing takes a three-hour time span. Do you know how much stuff you can get done in a three-hour time span? And is it worth throwing the kids off their schedule and paying a babysitter? Maybe it is, but usually the guilt costs you more. You reason that it's a lot easier to stay home and maybe get in an exercise video sometime during the evening after the kids are in bed . . . if you're not too beat. In other words, you won't be exercising anytime soon. And really, the guilt of going "out" wouldn't make you feel so bad if you didn't spend so much time away from your kids during the work week already.

So maybe you're really not giving yoga the full benefit of a doubt because the feelings of future guilt are clouding your judgement? Yep, very possible. You're just hoping your cousin doesn't confuse the jealousy tone in your voice for non-interest. So you make a little more of an effort to ask her a few more details before finding some excuse to hang up the phone. You gotta admit; kids are a great excuse!

After hanging up the phone, you start thinking about these crazy jealous feelings of yours! Really, feeling guilty about wishing you could leave your kids sometimes without feeling guilty. Okay, get a life. Your husband was right; you do need to get out.

❖

Tip #21–Enough Guilt Already.

Yes, working mom, there is such a thing as too much guilt. How do you get rid of it? I don't think it's actually possible to get rid of it, but perhaps learning to live with it is a more realistic realisation.

Everyone deals with different kinds of guilt and different levels of guilt, but it's a continual battle. Maybe that's really what estrogen is made up of; guilt hormones! And by the time you have a good handle on all that built-up guilt; the kids have long since grown-up and have kids of their own. And I'm guessing being a grandparent won't be any easier; it's probably another type of guilt altogether.

Author's Perspective
#1–We Do It to Ourselves.

It's funny how things work out. Women fought for the right to work out of the home. Then they fought for the right to compete against men for almost every work position available. Now, some women are fighting for the right to stay home and raise their families without getting slack from their husbands, friends, and society in general for not contributing financially to their family's well-being. Although it does seem that in today's economy, more and more women have no choice but to head back to work to try and help make ends meet.

Now, of course, every Mom works and every Mom experiences stress. Speaking from experience, working moms (and I mean the ones who also work out of the home) sometimes experience an over-whelming amount of stress that is often self-inflicted.

A lot of this stress comes from the unreasonable high expectations we place on ourselves to accomplish and achieve everything we set out to do. And why do we place such high expectations? What are we trying to prove? And who are we trying to prove it for?

There are many things that we can do to help make our lives easier as a working mom. There are several tips mentioned in this book to help you change your way of thinking and help make your life a little easier. What you'll really appreciate is the fact that you're not the only working mom out there trying to struggle through the guilt of pleasing everyone around you and forgetting about the most important person, *yourself*, because if you're not healthy and happy, you're no good to anyone else around you. Don't forget that you matter, too!

Superman has nothing on you, working mom. While he's continually flying around trying to save the world with all of that extra time he has on his hands, you've got a lot more to worry about. You're busy trying to put in a hard day's work (at your paid job) while trying to keep up with everything and everyone at home. This, of course, also has to be done with a smile on your face. How often do you see Superman smile?

#2-Years of Neglect

How much time passes by before we actually realize how much we've neglected ourselves? We're so busy putting everyone else ahead of ourselves that we forget that we're important too. Because we're so busy looking after everyone else, who's looking after us?

Sometimes when I see a woman take great pride in her appearance (you know the ones who can't leave the house without their make-up on and their hair done), I feel a little jealous. And I wonder why I am so comfortable leaving the house without make-up? I know it's not because I know I can get away with it. If I were still in my twenties, maybe, but not in my thirties. The normal "wear and tear" of a working mother is starting to show.

I guess it must not really be a priority for me. And that's obvious since it's not something I think about on the way out. I don't say, "Oh! I'm going to pick up the mail. I'd better put on some lipstick!" It's more or less, "I wonder if I should change my florescent pink sweat pants before going to pick up the mail in town? Nah, I shouldn't see anyone I know in the two minutes I'll be in there?" Come on, who really likes to dress up on their days off? It's nice to have some "down time" some-times, but of course, that is when I'm not only going to run into someone I know, but at least three people–including my neighbour, a co-worker, and a family friend. Great! Then I get mad at myself thinking that I should've burned those damn pants when I had the chance. Who doesn't have a favourite pair of pants that are so comfortable (obviously a little too comfortable) that you hold onto just for security. And really, why the hell do those pink pants make me feel so secure anyway?

I usually have seventeen other things on my mind as I'm heading out the door that anything regarding myself is put on the "back burner." Do I have all my kids? (Hey, as soon as there were more than two, I started doing headcounts.) Do I have the diaper bag? Are the wipes, diapers, and a bottle in there? Do I have hats, coats, and proper shoes for everyone? Do I need the stroller? Where did I put my cell phone? Do we need water and snacks? Do I need to fuel up? Are there a couple of extra blankets handy in case we need them? . . . and on and on. And this is only for an hour appointment in town. Anything regarding myself usually gets forgotten; like make-up or an extra coat. It's no wonder I don't like to go places on my days off, it's too much thinking. And I've done too much thinking this week at work already so that I'm exhausted by the time the weekend comes.

This is how easy it is to forget about yourself. I finally realized that amidst working for the past decade and putting my family first, I'm a tired, overweight, frumpy thirty-year-old mom. I think *frumpy* describes it best. I don't have time or money to keep up with the latest fashions. I know my kids come first and my needs always seem to be last on the list. And there is always something that the kids need that seems to take priority over my needs. The school fees, extracurricular activities, clothing, shoes, birthday gifts seem to come first. And why? That's mostly my own fault, I admit it. It also doesn't help that I've been saying I should lose twenty pounds before going shopping for new work clothes. And needless to say, if I keep up this attitude, I won't be shopping for a while because those twenty pounds seem to stick on stronger than dried cereal in a forgotten, breakfast bowl. (You know what I'm talking about!)

And I can't say that I'm a high-maintenance person. I'm not a "name-brand," "brand-name," "name-that-brand" kind of girl. I'll admit it, I love garage sales! It's a rush to find something you can use at home at a bargain price. And the fun of garage sales is you never know what you're going to find? Although, I prefer to shop at the ones I know are going to have kids' clothes and toys, not the ones that sell used underwear and broken microwaves (yes, some people try to sell anything). And I'll admit that I don't enjoy putting them on as much (they're a lot of work and require a lot of time), but it's nice to stop in at one for five minutes on your way home from work. The kids seem to really enjoy them too, especially when we find something they can play with outside when we get home.

I'm getting off-track. My point is I know I don't have to spend a fortune on myself. I just have to learn to take the time to take care of myself. The hardest part of this challenge is not to feel guilty about taking time away from the kids. When I've been away all week from them, it's really hard to say, "Sorry guys; I've got to leave for a couple of hours and go to the gym." That's not going to happen. Through experience, I've learned to be creative and exercise by playing ball with them or taking them for walks in the stroller while my older ones ride their bikes. They really enjoy it, and admittedly I do too when I get into it. Taking the time to shave my legs more than once a month or plucking my eyebrows and putting on make-up religiously is hard to do. I'm just not used to it. I'm sure that once I establish a regular weekly routine, it should get easier. When do I have time to start a new routine?

I know it's easy to make excuses and blame everyone else for not looking after myself. I've done it myself and who hasn't heard, "Oh, I just got so busy, I didn't have time to exercise. No, I never have a chance to make a really healthy meal because I always work late. The kids keep me so busy, I forget about me." And it admittedly gets really dull hearing from the same people over and over again. You hear that, annoying people? You get on my nerves! You just have to learn to admit, like me, that it's your own fault you're not feeling great about yourself. Blaming it on the kids, work, or your husband gets old. And people get tired of hearing the same old story? Admit it; you're fat because you let yourself get fat. "Baby fat" (you know, that nice little tire around the middle) is only an excuse for so long. Ten years later, you can't hide behind that baby-fat excuse, which is actually lazy, flabby, belly fat.

Now admitting it is the easy part, but the hardest part is doing something about it. I really planned on doing something about it in my twenties. Then, all of a sudden, I turned thirty and realized that I was still planning to do something about it. Realistically, forty will creep up on me and I'll be kicking myself in the ass for not doing something about it sooner. Actually, kicking myself in the ass would probably be a good form of exercise. I wonder what the calorie burn would be?

Although, I'm a working mom, I can't forget to remind myself on a daily basis, of how lucky I am. working moms are so busy being pulled in ten different directions that it's easy to forget how lucky we are to have a loving partner, happy, healthy kids, and a job that pays the bills. Not everyone can say that. Sometimes it doesn't hurt to thank the Big Guy upstairs once in a while.

#3–Bitchy Women?

Now I talked a lot about our physical well-being, but what about a working mom's mental well-being? Of course we know that they're interconnected because your physical well-being will lead to your mental well-being.

When I started my first part-time job in high school, I was full of piss and vinegar. Trying to balance school, homework, job, sports, and a social life got pretty hectic. Sure, my school work suffered some, but it was also a lot of fun and I was a kid who liked to keep busy. Work then was kind of like my "Yes sir, yes ma'am" work days. I worked hard to please the boss and did whatever anyone told me. I didn't question what I was supposed to do, and I understood that doing the hard or tedious jobs were expected since I was the lowest on the totem pole. Minimum wage and sometimes crappy hours were part of the package. I was a hard worker; I learned a lot about finances and managed to get along with most all of my co-workers.

One of things I learned was budgeting. I really had to save up to purchase anything extravagant; therefore, if I really wanted that $80 pair of jeans, I had to save a week's worth of wages to pay for them. I quickly learned that maybe name-brand jeans weren't a necessity, as I had previously thought, for a teenage girl who wanted to look "cool." Or if I still really wanted them, I started looking for coupons or a good sale before considering purchasing them.

It's funny how if you make more money, you spend more money. And it's so true, even if you don't intentionally mean to. Sure, the more kids you have, the more purchases, like clothing and groceries, there is to buy. If you don't make it, you don't spend it–unless you start buying things on credit, but that's a whole other self-help book and not my area of expertise.

As I got older, some things changed. Besides making more money, I still worked hard and got along with my co-workers, but I also learned to start standing up for myself. I don't know if it comes with experience, age, or having children, but something definitely changes. I no longer allow myself to get walked on or if I am put in an awkward position or not treated fairly, I learned to question my supervisor for an explanation.

I've often heard the famous expression "bitchy women at work." Yes, I totally agree that sometimes women can be bitchy. Now, whether it's for the right or the wrong reason, it's hard to say. I will say that women seem to get more protective after they start a family. They start looking after the best interests of them and their family members and not only what's good for the boss. So if they chose not to work overtime because they'd rather be home with their kids or refuse to take on any more extra work because they already feel overwhelmed, I don't know if I can call that *bitchy*. I think I'd call that *protective*. Understandably, if they continue to stir up problems at work and refuse to help find a solution, I'd have to say the "bitch-o-meter" is not leaning in their favour.

Now, I've worked in offices with only women, and I've also worked in offices with only men. Do I do agree that working with 100 men is easier than working in an office with only ten women? Maybe sometimes, but I'll admit that men's crudeness, sense of humour, and their ability to be blunt can be hard to handle sometimes. It is definitely a plus not to have to deal with their PMS.

I think one of the biggest stresses on working women have is trying to keep up with everyone else's expectations. From experience, I know that letting anyone down is not part of my plan. I would rather stress myself out trying to make things work-whether it's scheduling, finances, or something else-than let people down.

I had a funny discussion with my grandma a while back. It went something like this:

"I don't know how you moms of today do it?"

"What do you mean, mémère?" What did my grandma mean by that?

"I don't know how you young moms can be so busy?"

I was perplexed. This comment was coming from a Mom who raised eleven children in the 1940s and 1950s; a Mom of eleven children whose husband was a logger and often worked away for months at a time; a Mom of eleven children who didn't have a washing machine, dish washer, or running water, for that matter. And she didn't know how we did it? Bless her soul.

It's easy to see the physical affects after years of forgetting about ourselves, but our mental well-being is just as fragile.

I guess Moms, especially working moms, are built to handle whatever comes their way. We are made to do the best we can to love, nurture, and satisfy our family's needs and wants (to a certain extent because my son is still not getting a race car). I think we'd better learn to have a little more faith in our abilities and appreciate our willingness to always do what's best for those around us. And the most important point is to set reasonable expectations and not set the bar so damn high.

#4–Personal Note

There's not much I can complain about. I was privileged to have grown up in a two-parent household with hardworking parents, a roof over my head, and food in my belly.

While growing up, I never remember being left with a babysitter regularly or having any after-school care. My parents were business owners and therefore, were fortunate enough to have been able to work their schedules around our schedules. My mom stayed home with my sister, brother, and me throughout the morning while my dad was at work (he started his shift very early in the morning). Once my dad would come home around nap time, where he would usually be able to grab a little shut-eye himself, my mom would go to work and close-up shop. My mom was able to stay at home and didn't work outside the home until all of us kids were in school. I remember family suppers, family outings, and church on Sundays. We weren't rich, but we were by no means poor. I never remember going without something we needed. Sure, sometimes we went without something we wanted, like a pony for instance, but that's understandable. I know my parents sometimes went without, like forgoing purchasing a new winter coat for themselves because school fees came first, but they did a great job of hiding it. They also did a great job teaching us family and religious values, good work ethics, and how to appreciate the little things.

It was only later growing up that we heard some of their hard-luck stories of trying to raise a family on a limited income. Some of the stories including starting a business in the 1980s at twenty-one percent interest and succeeding. Of course, many of their payments over the years went straight to interest charges with nothing bringing down the principal amount; yet, Santa was still able to bring "ghetto-blasters" and Cabbage Patch dolls for Christmas that year. Nowadays, if interest ever hit twenty-one percent again, most of our population would go bankrupt.

Other stories included my dad quitting school at seventeen and moving out to go and work for a living because my grandparents couldn't afford to have him stay at home. And one of my all-time favourites is a story that involves how my parents lied about their financial situation at one bank to allow them to obtain money for a family holiday. Now this "family holiday" was actually down payment on a home. Of course, the bank will not lend you money for the down payment. Therefore, once the funds for the "family holiday" were processed, they walked with the money for their down payment in hand to their other bank across the street where their home-owner's loan was being handled. My parents did their best to provide for my sister, brother, and me. Although, I don't think I ever gave them enough credit for their creativity.

Why is it, as parents, we're always trying to give our kids more, more, more? Why do we think they need more than we had growing up? Do they really need that trip to Disneyland, those name-brand clothes, or that new car at age sixteen? Do they really need *that* or do we think they really want that? And do they really want that because we've put it in their heads that it's important to have nice, tangible things.

So we've put this pressure on ourselves to continue supplying our kids with such great stuff. We work more overtime to pay for hockey lessons; we work on weekends to pay for the new house we think we need; and we work on holidays to pay for the new motor home for our family camp-outs.

And so, how much are we using that family motor home we so

desperately needed when we're working during the holidays anyway? And how often are we home on weekends to enjoy our new home when we're so busy working to pay for it? And why is it so important to push our kids to play sports that we wished ourselves we could've played when we were growing up? I guess the point is, is it really important to them, or is it really important to us? Keeping up with the Jones' is hard enough, never mind trying to keep up to the Thompsons, the Simpsons, and the Tucketts as well.

I'm not saying quitting your job is what you should do, working mom. I'm just saying that sometimes downsizing or staying within a realistic budget can relieve a lot of financial pressure and perhaps alleviate some of the work-related stress that comes with working outside the home. You have to decide what's really important. After all, you have to think about what you want it to say on your gravestone when you're gone . . . "Here lies our happy, healthy, loving mom" or "Here lies our stressed-out, crabby, tired mom who meant well, but never really got it"?

#5–Putting Things in Perspective

Don't forget that you have a lot to be thankful for. You have to count your blessings because there are so many. Having a father that didn't let me rely on self-pity sure helped make me appreciate what I had. I think I heard "It could be worse" at least once a week growing up.

"Dad, I wish my eyes were blue, not green."

"At least you can see out of them, not everyone can. It could be worse."

"Dad, I wish I didn't have this cold in my sinuses."

"At least it's temporary. Our neighbour just found out she has cancer. It could be worse."

"Dad, I wish we could afford to go to Disneyland."

"At least we're able to afford food, shelter, and that brand-new bike you wanted. Not everyone has a hot pink BMX. It could be worse."

It could be worse . . . it could be worse . . . it could be worse . . .

He was always willing to put things in perspective. No matter how bad my situation seemed, there was always somebody who had bigger problems. Sometimes, however, I just wanted a little pity, especially when I was a teenager having a bad day. Okay, I'm sure I received a little pity ever now and then, but that's not what stuck with me now.

Who are we to complain when we are so blessed (even though we are human)? Health and happiness are the basis of a prosperous life. Sometimes, it just takes a while for people to realize that or for somebody to point it out to them. I am truly thankful that I am able to have a family of my own. Not everyone can say that. It's important to keep that in mind the next time your kids are driving you crazy.

And you should never underestimate the power of positive thinking.

I truly believe that positive thinking affects your quality of life. Sure, things aren't always going to be in your favour, but there's usually a silver lining in that cloud somewhere.

I find it amazing as to how much of an impact my parents had on me. It became very obvious when I started quoting them. Walking into my home, it's very possible to hear . . .

"Mom, I wish I had brand new hockey skates."

"Son, you're lucky you're able to play hockey. Lots of families can't afford it. It could be worse."

We have to remember how much influence we have on our kids. They're like little sponges waiting to soak up whatever it is you want to teach them. And sometimes they're such great learners that they even pick up stuff you don't even realize that you're teaching them–bad habits and all.

All in all, I guess my mom and dad must have done a pretty good job. I have to remember to thank them!

About the Author

Like a lot of students, I was unable to pick out specifically where I wanted to end up after high school. Therefore, I decided to enroll in a Business Management Program in 1997. I knew I wanted to have a good understanding of management basics that would help me wherever I worked.

After successfully obtaining my diploma and working a few years in the oil patch and as a court clerk, I married my high school sweetheart in 2000. It was only after having my first child that I realized that I wanted to pursue my teaching degree. This would allow me to work with kids in a positive environment. I hoped to help shape kids' ideals instead of being a witness to the aftermath of their wrongdoings as a court clerk. My hard work paid off in 2004 when I received my teaching degree.

After dipping my toes in my new career, our second son was born in 2005. Two kids were a lot of work, but two kids and a career was even harder to juggle. Nevertheless, I continued to work and run the kids around. This was in-between moving a couple times, until we eventually ended up back on the farm where my husband grew up. In between farming and my husband working as a welder, and as well as trying to squeeze in family time around my work schedule, our daughter then followed in 2008.

Although it's been a busy maternity leave, I was happy to be able to write personal life experiences, as well as those shared by other working moms. As a first-time writer, I am convinced these stories need to be told. And why not tell these stories while getting a good laugh. We could all use it!

LaVergne, TN USA
04 January 2011
211059LV00008BC/176/P

JAN 2 8 2011